I0481969

# SEO for Growth

# The Ultimate Guide to Learn Search Engine Optimization with Internet Marketing Tips

**LELA GIBSON**

LELA GIBSON

# CONTENTS

# Introduction

I want to thank you and congratulate you for buying the book, *"SEO for Growth: The Ultimate Guide to Learn Search Engine Optimization with Internet Marketing Tips"*.

This book has actionable information that will help you to understand SEO like a pro.

Search Engine Optimization (SEO) is the aspect of ensuring a web property, be it a web article, video, or image, appears relevant to specific keywords search engine users use when using the various search engines to search for specific/related information. It is also about placing these keywords at strategic areas of the web property so that search engines can easily recognize the nature of the web property and rank it accordingly.

SEO, although it sounds complex, is actually not and once you learn what to do and not to do as you optimize your web property, your online marketing plan shall start paying dividends fast.

In this SEO guide, we are going to simplify everything SEO and show you how to implement search engine optimization to your internet-marketing plan so you can reap immense benefits from the large marketplace that is the internet. Let's begin.

Thanks again for buying this book. I hope you enjoy it!

# Is SEO Dead?

Whenever two or more SEOs meet up (SEOs is the name given to those who specialize in search engine optimization), they will discuss the notion of the death of SEO and whether investing in it is a wise choice.

Let us dispense with this question right now.

## SEO is not dead!

Yes, Google—the largest search engine by users—may have rolled out search algorithms updates that make SEO seemingly difficult. However, if done right, SEO could be the difference between getting eyeballs on your web property (and thus increasing your chances of converting these eyeballs into direct sales) or no eyeballs at all, which in the internet marketing space means oblivion.

If SEO is not dead, and if done right, can yield great results, what should you do to optimize your web property for search engines? The answer to this is simple: **nothing.** Before you bite my head off for being so blasphemous, let me explain.

## *Why You Should Not Optimize For Search Engines*

If you read Google's mission statement (in this SEO book, we are going to concentrate on Google optimization simply because Google is the largest search engine), you will notice that Google has a very simple mission:

*"To organize the world's information and make it universally accessible and useful."*

This mission statement is why you should not optimize for search engines and should instead optimize your web property for users. Here is why:

Long gone are the days when stuffing keywords on a website's title tag or Meta description tricked the spiders at Google into considering this site relevant to that specific keyword and thus giving it first rank. Google has consistently rolled out algorithm updates that have made their search spiders (not actual spiders of course☺) immensely intelligent.

Today, other than looking at keyword gravity, search engines are using other metrics such as page speed, bounce rates, and quality links to determine if a site or content on a site is going to help them achieve their mission statement: *help users by organizing the internet to ensure readers only get results relevant to their search criteria.*

Therefore, instead of optimizing for search spiders, you should optimize for user, which as you may have guessed, would put you in Google's good grace because when you do this, you are helping them achieve their mission statement, which at the very core of it, *is being the most helpful (to users) search engine on the planet.*

That is why you should not concentrate on optimizing for search engines and instead, concentrate on optimizing for real user/people. There is a caveat to this.

Even though you should optimize for users, you should also optimize for search engines to ensure search engine spiders consider your site/web property relatable to a specific keyword/s so they can give you a good rank. How do you do this? How do you make sure real life users find your website amazingly accessible and helpful while at the same time making sure you tweak your website to make it search engine friendly. Teaching you how to do that is the purpose of this book.

Before we get to that, let us look at the importance of search engine optimization from a marketing perspective.

# Why Search Engine Optimization Is an Integral Part of Internet Marketing

Many small businesses and online entrepreneurs often wonder why they should invest time and money (in some instances) into search engine optimization. The answer to this is very simple: *search engine optimization could make or break a business.*

At the time of writing this book, almost half of earth's population uses the internet: that is over 3.2 billion people. Now, as a perceptive businessperson, to have a thriving business, how many of these users would you need to capture and turn into buyer and brand ambassadors?

Suppose you are the proud owner of a "car seat affiliate site" or "an online shop." Obviously, to make your site profitable, you would have to target a specific section of the 3.2 billion people using the internet. How do you know which people to target? You do something called **keyword research**. What is keyword research? To define this, we need to understand what keywords are:

Keywords are what the name suggests: **key words**. In relation to SEO and its importance, keywords are the phrases and words search engine users type into their respective search boxes when searching for specific information. From an internet marketing perspective, keywords are the topics and ideas (in terms of the words appearing on your web property) that define the nature of your website in relation to the topic it covers.

Keyword research is whereby you or your SEO professional go about finding which keywords and phrases (and their alternatives) users are inputting into their search boxes when searching for information on a specific topic related to the subject your website covers. The aim of researching these keywords is to use them on your web copy, image, video, or otherwise to show Google and other search engines the relevancy of your web property to a specific subject, which means because it is relevant and helpful to users, Google will give your website a better rank.

In the example above, to determine which segment of the 3.2 billion people search for car seats or the product offerings on your online store, you would need to conduct keyword research. This is what SEO does: *it gives your marketing direction because when you know whom you are targeting, you are better equipped to provide this user/s with the exact information they seek.* Targeting at this level has many advantages.

For one, it means because you will have discovered your target audience, your marketing efforts shall stop being shots in the dark: *you will have a targeted focus.* This has implications in that when you are not 'winging your marketing,' you are bound to yield better marketing results and obviously, better sales.

Another thing is that unlike other marketing channels such as magazine advertisement and banner ads that cost an arm and a leg, SEO is comparably cheaper and much more effective because once you do it, you will only have to tweak it accordingly. Additionally, once you get the traffic flowing to your site where you can impress users with your amazingly helpful content, users are bound to love your site and content, which translates into raving fans and because of tis, Google and other search engines are bound to shower love and attention on your web property. This translates into better ranking and more eyeballs on your property.

Another important reason why you should concentrate on SEO is the mere fact that SEO has a multiplicity effect. For instance, going with our car seat example, if you create the ultimate car buying seat resource, a resource that trumps all other available resources, Google will not only reward you with first page ranking (provided you do other things such as optimization and back linking), you will also be helping users. The first rule of making money from the internet, which is what internet marketing is all about, is *be helpful.*

When users consider your car seat resource 'the ultimate go to guide,' they are bound to take up your recommendations because they shall start considering you an authority in that market. This translates into better sales.

Further, when you create the best resource for whichever segment of the market you are targeting, your resource is bound to go viral especially when you consider that today, when users find something useful, they are more than willing to share it on their social media profiles. This has a viral multiplication effect that can set your web property up for immense success.

Another important thing to note here is that social shares are also a ranking factor simply because when users share your content, it tells Google that your content is helpful to its users. You can guess what this means to your SERP ranking (SERP means search engine results page).

We cannot fail to mention the credibility aspect. Search engine optimization has the ability to turn small businesses into brands worth following. At the core of branding is the need to increase the number of people who know of the existence of your business. In this, SEO and branding are mutually exclusive through link building.

The very nature and reason for building link, as shown in the image below, is to create brand awareness to a point where your business (what we call a brand) is top of the mind of each of your target audience.

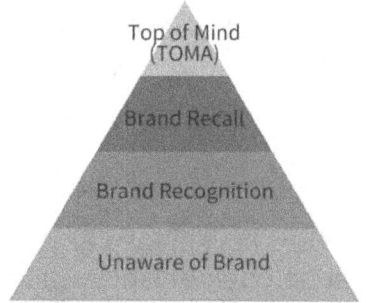

This happens because when you optimize your content and site (using strategically located keywords and back linking) whenever your target audience types into their search box the keywords you have optimized for, your website/brand/business is going to rank first for these keywords (i.e. assuming your content is out-of-this-world good and you create naturally occurring backlinks). When you rank first for specific keywords, prospects are bound to believe you are the best, which is bound to increase your brand recognition.

Another advantage of engaging in SEO is that unlike other marketing strategy that have a short-lived nature, SEO is a long-term marketing strategy in the following sense.

When you invest in an advertising strategy such as buying ads be it on Facebook, Google, or other PPC advertising model, what you are truly investing your money is short term return on investment. Do not derive this to mean PPC and other marketing strategies are not great ways to drive traffic to your web property, they are. However, compared to SEO, natural search results always trump paid advertising channels because when search engine users have the option of choosing an ad on the first page of SERP over a natural search result, they will always go for the latter.

When properly optimized through white hat SEO hacks such as natural keyword placements instead of spammy keyword placement, natural link building to quality sites, and other optimization strategies such as optimizing page speed, mobile friendliness, and bounce rate, a web page or article ranked first on Google can stay there for a substantial amount of time. When you compare this to an instance where another marketer can outbid your ad, SEO is a better prospect especially when you take into account that SEO works long after you commit the initial optimization work.

Now that we have looked at the importance of SEO as an integral part of your internet marketing strategy, you may be wondering, "Which SEO aspects should I concentrate on to get the biggest bang for my buck?" The answer to this is three fold: you need to concentrate on **keyword research**, which includes creating great keyword optimized copy, **link building**, which includes natural, quality back links and social shares and signals, and **site optimization**, which include page load speed, mobile friendliness, bounce rate, and other important metrics.

To make the rest of this SEO guide an easy follow, we are going to look at two of these factors: keyword research and link building, and as we do so, throw in ties for site optimization. Let us start with keyword research.

# The Ultimate Keyword Research Guide

Keywords are the backbone of every SEO campaign; without them, SEO would not exist. Here is why. Even though search engines have continued to evolve with every algorithm update, they still rely on keywords to determine the nature of a web property and the topic it discusses.

Keyword research helps you determine which keywords to use as you create your content, how to create this content (taking into account keyword placement) in a way that is appealing to search engine users and search engine spiders, and the strategic places to place these keywords for maximum effectiveness.

In truth, how we (SEOs) conduct keyword research has not changed much. What has changed is how we use these keywords to optimize our web properties. To optimize your website and content for search, you need to conduct keyword research but instead of spamming keywords all over your website, you need to be strategic about the prospect so you can avoid Google penalties such as site de-ranking.

In this book, we shall not go into the details of how to conduct keyword research because the internet is chockfull of actionable content that shall teach you how to conduct keyword research like a pro. In the off chance that you would like to brush up your keyword research knowledge, the links below will give you an updated version of how to do keyword research:

Backlinko.com/

Moz.com

What we shall do here is outline where and how to use keywords for maximum effectiveness in relation to internet marketing.

## Where to Place Keywords

This part of the guide shall assume you have used the links above to generate a healthy mix of short-tail and long-tail keywords and are ready to use them. Now that you have this, the next part of the process is to figure out where to use these keywords to ensure your increase possibilities of 1st SERP ranking.

To do this, we shall concentrate on what most marketers call on-page optimization. On-page optimization is anything you do on your website, content, images, videos, etc. to improve your website relevancy in the eyes of search engine spiders with the aim being to improve search ranking. Without proper on-page optimization, anything else you do off-page, which is where something such as external link building comes in, will all be for naught.

To use keywords to optimize (on-page) your web property, here are the central areas you should pay attention to:

**CRUCIALLY IMPORTANT NOTE: DO NOT** overdo keyword optimization. Remember that Google and other search engines hate keyword stuffing: they see this as an attempt at subterfuge. If you are spammy with your keyword placement, you can bet your SEOs ass that Google is going to relegate your website to the last page of search results. Have you ever been to the last page of Google SERP? No one ever goes there. Instead of being spammy with your keywords, lay them out naturally and rather than use one keyword, use several related keyword phrases.

When you naturally place keywords at the following strategic locations, your rank will improve:

**Title Tag:** Title tags are the element of your website search engine crawlers use to determine the nature and subject of your page or content. Google displays 50-60 characters of the title tag. Ideally, when curating your title tag, you should ensure the title tag has your brand or business names and all the main keywords you would like that page to rank for.

Placement for this tag is between the <HEAD> </HEAD> tags at the top of the HTML code for the page.

**Meta Description:** After scanning the title tag, web crawlers then head over to the Meta description to learn more about the nature of your page. The Meta description is the information appearing below webpage search results for keywords users' type into their Google search boxes.

While some SEOs opine that Meta descriptions have little to no bearing on ranking, it is good practice to optimize your Meta description with keywords. As you do this, keep in mind the human element because users shall use this to determine if a page or content on a page is relevant to the information they seek.

**HACK:** If you are using a CMS (content management system) such as WordPress, you can use SEO plugins such as SEO by Yoast or All in One SEO to optimize your title tags and Meta description without having to go into your website's source code. This is especially beneficial if you know very little about HTML and CSS.

**Header Tags:** The most commonly used Header tags, or HTML tags range from H1>H6. These ones are especially effective when used to break up content into pieces that give search engines an opportunity to learn what each aspect of the section covers. Title tags are also ideal places to use a mix of keyword related to your main keyword.

Whenever you are using these tags, only use the <H1></H1> tag once on a post or page simply because this tag surrounds a post or page title. As for the others (H2 to H6 and beyond) you can use them as you see fit to break up content in a way that makes reading it easier for your web visitors including crawlers.

**ALT tags and Image Name:** Search engines cannot directly index videos or images. Therefore, to ascertain the nature of the images and videos you have used on your website and web copy, they depend on image name and ALT tags. Optimize the images and videos you place on a page or post by using relevant keywords for the name and title tag so that Google can relate these images and videos to your website topic. This will improve your search ranking.

**Content:** Keywords should also make an appearance on your web copy. Unfortunately, this is where most marketers go crazy and spam the content with keywords thus making it unreadable for users. Remember what we have consistently stated in this book: *the more you spam keywords, the heftier Google's punishment, and the lower your ranking shall be.*

Instead of spamming keywords into your copy, come up with a long list of relevant short tail and long tail keywords and use these as naturally as you can within your copy. Ideally, if placing a keyword somewhere compromises readability, do not insert such a keyword. The key idea here is to be helpful to readers.

However, in instances where you can do so naturally, place your main keywords within the first 100 words of your copy and use related keywords for the title tags. You can also benefit from placing your main keyword/s within the last 10 words of the closing paragraph.

In terms of content length, many SEOs are yet to agree on the ideal content length for optimal ranking. However, one thing most do agree on is that you should use as many or as few words as you need to ensure the content you create is helpful to readers. If 1,000 words are all you need, good, go for it. If you need 3,000, go for it. Just ensure the content you create is helpful to readers because at the core of SEO is concentrating on what search engine users are searching for.

In relation to the word count, read the following blogs to see what Neil Patel and Nickie Bartels, two highly experienced SEOs have to say about content length and its effect on ranking:

Quicksprout.com

Blog.influenceandco.com

Now that we have looked at everything keyword research and optimization, let us look at the other part: link building.

# Link Building in: How to Build Quality Links

In more instances than one, Google has clearly stated that links are one of the main factors they use to rank webpages and content. As we stated in earlier section of this guide, back links (quality ones) cement your brand and when many people are linking back to your content (this include sharing the content on social media), this tells Google that information contained in your content or web page is important to users.

Here is the thing; links are not equal. If you have low quality, spam like sites linking back to your site, Google shall conclude that your content and website is also spammy and therefore, it will devalue your page and content. This therefore means that even as you seek to create back links, you should only create quality back links because doing otherwise will leave your internet-marketing plan in limbo.

To create quality backlinks, you need to concentrate on one very important element before you can even start using the various link building strategies we shall discuss here to prospect for quality backlinks.

## Content: Get It Right!

In the early days of SEO, SEOs could get away with creating low quality, keyword stuffed content and still manage to rank well even if the content they were creating was not relevant to the keywords they were using on their content.

There is a very popular analogy of how in the early days of SEO, SEOs could optimize their content in such a manner that when granny searched for "home care," the resulting links on the first page of Google could take her to an "escort site." Those days are long gone. Today, if you create spammy content, Google will consider you spam and de-rank you.

Before you start prospecting for backlinks, make sure your content is top notch because after a thousand algorithm updates, content is still king and when you create great content, content Google users love, the search gods will reward you with better ranking. In actuality, when you create top-notch, award-winning copy, you will not have to work very hard to generate backlinks: *other web masters will want to link back to you simply because your content is the best possible.*

Do not fall into the trap of thinking search crawlers are dumb robots and thus, have no way of telling if content is of high quality. If you fall into this trap and create spin articles, you will be doing yourself a disservice because although you will be directing time and resources into content creation, all your effort shall be for naught. Before you can even think about creating links, you need to get your content right.

Learning how to create great content is a lengthy topic that deserves a book on its own. For now, head over to the link below to learn a thing or two about creating content Google loves and that ranks well:

Neilpatel.com

# Link Building Strategies for Internet Marketing

Once you know your content is great, you can get started on link building. To do this, you can implement various strategies. Let us discuss the most effective of these strategies:

## 1: The Guest Posting Strategy

Guest posting is still one of the most effective, white hack way to create backlinks. The best thing about this strategy is that on top of buffing up your backlink profile, it also leads to increased traffic. Here is why.

If you concentrate on guest blogging on niche relevant authority sites, and your content on these sites is great, naturally, readers shall want to know more about you and because you will have a link pointing back to your website, these readers will hop to your website to read some more of your awesome content.

Here, you need to reach out to bloggers that curate content relevant to your niche and promise to add value to their blogs by creating user helpful content. This is one of the best ways to create a great back link profile.

When talking about guest blogging, we cannot fail to mention content syndication as a way to beef up your backlink profile.

Content syndication revolves around publishing one piece of content (great content) on multiple blogs. While this may sound spammy, it is not and most large publications have dedicated syndication networks that allow them to work with websites in the same niche to republish trending content. Whenever, a syndication network republishes content, the networks give credit to the author and in some instances (most instances actually) link back to the partner's (your) website.

Content syndication is a fantastic way to get your content published on popular blogs on the internet (meaning because they are popular, Google considers them to have a high domain authority), and get quality backlinks pointing back to your site especially when the content syndication sites allow you to have a featured author bio.

## 2: The Skyscraper Technique

Coined by Brian Dean of backlinko.com, this link building is one of the most effective ones there is; it is so effective that Brian used it to increase his traffic and grow his links by 106.9%. What is the skyscraper technique?

The skyscraper technique is a 3-step process.

### Step 1:

Find an amazing piece of proven linkable asset (this is fancy SEO lingo for niche specific content that is already popular and doing very well in its niche). For instance, if you are in the car seat niche, and are looking for linkable assets, you just have to head to Google and type in your target keywords, the ones you would like to rank for. The content that shows up in the first page of SERP counts as linkable asset.

### Step 2:

Outdo this amazing content by creating something superior albeit with a similar messaging. This is very important because that content has already proven effective and if you create something better, with a little hard work, you are bound to end out ranking this content.

## Step 3:

Once they create great copy, most internet marketers leave it that, cross their fingers, and hope that Google shall recognize their amazing content and rank it first. Unfortunately, things never work out in this manner and to signal Google and tell it "hey, I published content worth ranking first," you have to engage in outreach and marketing

Brian recommends email outreach. In email outreach, you find influencers in your niche. The idea here is to show these influencers how valuable the content you have created shall be to their readers. Obviously, this can only work if you reach out to the right people: *you should not email random people.* Instead, reach out to site owners whose content links out to content similar to the content you have created. This means the persons you reach out to should have a site in your niche, be interested in your topic, and have linked to the topic your article discusses.

Below is the email outreach Brian Dean recommends and has used to grow his links.

---

Hey [Name],

I was searching for some articles about [Your topic] today and I came across this page: [URL]

I noticed that you linked to one of my favorite articles-- [Article Title]

Just wanted to give you a heads up that I created a similar. It's like [Name of the article], but more thorough and up to date: [URL]

Might be worth a mention on your page.

Either way, keep up the awesome work!

Cheers,
[Your name]

---

## 3: The Broken Link Building Technique

We have already established that backlinks are a super important Google ranking feature. Broken link building is one of the tested and tried ways to generate back links because instead of, in relation to the above strategy, "begging for links," you are adding value to someone's website. In this strategy, here is what you do:

The first thing you need to do install a broken link checker such as My Links or LinkMiner (these two are Google Chrome extensions). These tools allow you to find broken links on a page without having to navigate away from your browser or log into a software.

Once you have this installed, the next step is to find pages that have a healthy outbound links profile. The more a page links to other pages, the higher the likelihood that it will have broken links. If you are unsure about which pages to view, you can never go wrong with resource pages. To find resource pages related to your niche, use the following search strings:

*"Keyword" + inurl:links*

*"Keyword" + "helpful resources"*

*"Keyword" + "useful resources"*

*"Keyword" + "useful links"*

Replace *"Keyword"* with your niche specific keyword:

At this point, run the extension to reveal the broken links on the page. Once you view the broken links (LinkMiner highlights them in red and all you have to do is scroll down the page), all you have to do know is email the site owner informing him or her of the broken link. Here is where you pitch the site owner the amazing content you created while using the previous strategy.

Below is the script Brian Dean (this is one of his favorite back linking strategy) uses for this strategy. Although tested and proven to work, you can customize this script accordingly:

**Subject: Problem with** [Their Site's Name]

—

Hi [Name],

Are you still updating your site?

I was searching for content on [Topic] when I came across your excellent page: [Page Title or URL].

However, I noticed a few links didn't seem to be working:

[URLs of broken links]

Also, I recently published [Brief Content Pitch]. It may make a good replacement for the [Point Out a Specific Broken Link].

Either way, I hope this helped you out ☺

Thanks,
[Your Name]

## 4: Resource Page Link Building

Resource pages are pages whose purpose is to link out to awesome content on any given topic: that is their sole purpose: to link out to other content. This makes them great prospects for link building.

To get started with this strategy, use the search strings in the previous strategy. Once you have these pages (several of them), size each one individually and ask yourself, "Would liking to this page be worthwhile?"

If the resource page has a great URLRating and great domain authority, you have a winner. Your next task is to find the best content fit for that specific resource page. When the content you want to add to the resource page fits like a glove, use the following script to reach out to the webmaster but customize it accordingly:

**Subject: Question about** [Their Website]

—

Hi [Name],

I was Googling around for content about [Topic] this morning, when I came across your excellent resource page: [URL].

I just wanted to say that your page helped me a ton. I would have never found the [Resource They Link To] without it.

It's funny: I recently published a guide on [Topic] last month. It's [Brief Description].

Here it is in case you'd like to check it out: [URL].

Also, my guide might make a nice addition to your page.

Either way, thanks for putting together your list of resources. And have a great day!

Talk Soon,

[Your Name]

With these 4 strategies, you are going to generate tons of backlinks to your website or content thus improving your backlink profile, traffic, and above all, ranking.

Keyword optimization on your page and in your content and link building are the two important things you need to do to skyrocket your ranking and traffic.

# Off-Page SEO Marketing Techniques

Search engine optimization is typically divided into two major categories- on-page, and off-page SEO.

On-Page SEO includes link building, keyword research, Meta tags, and all the other techniques mentioned earlier. Basically, on-page SEO refers to all the things you do within your website/blog to help you rank higher in search engines.

Off-Page SEO on the other hand, refers to things that you do outside your website/blog to increase your page rankings on search engines.

## Why Off-Page SEO is Important

The most important goal for search engines is generating the best search results to their users, and in order to achieve this goal, they often take both on-page and off-page SEO factors into consideration.

Off-page SEO gives an indication of how the rest of the world perceives your website. It is believed that when a website contains useful, high-quality content, other websites and users will reference it, there will be a lot of mentions of the site on social media and forums, the website would be bookmarked a lot, and contents of the website will be shared amongst the internet community.

A successful SEO strategy must include both on-site and off-site SEO techniques. Off-page SEO will help to increase your web traffic, increase your search engine page ranking, and give your website more exposure. So which techniques can you use? Here are some ideas:

## Off-Page SEO Techniques

1. **Social Networking Sites:** Improving your social media reputation is one of the biggest steps you can take towards building your off-page SEO. Here is how to go about it:

**Step 1:** Sign up on popular social networking sites, especially Facebook, Instagram, Twitter, Google Plus, etc. You have to create a dedicated profile for your business/blog on those social networks to make it look more professional. Make sure to fill your profile adequately; including your 'about', your contacts, opening hours, closing hours, timeline photos etc. You can then use your social media presence to generate leads and create awareness about your business page.

**Step 2**: Cross-promote your website/blog. This means you should build your network on social media by gathering a lot of followers, and then use your social media account to direct traffic to your web content. Also, place social sharing buttons on your blog, and encourage your web visitors to share the contents on your blog with their friends on Social media.

Don't just create a dormant social media page; make it interesting, and educational with a lot of useful contents that your friends and followers can share.

It also helps to interact with other bloggers or businesses in your niche. All of these further help to build your reputation and ranking online.

2. **Forum Marketing**: You can also use forum marketing to build your search engine ranking and online reputation.

Search for forums that are related to your niche and get involved with the community. Answering people's questions, offering helpful advice, and replying to threads can help you build a solid reputation for your website. Here is how to go about it:

**Step 1**: Search for "Do-follow" forums that are related to your site's niche.

**Step 2**: Look for questions you can answer, or threads that you can contribute to, and craft intelligent and helpful responses to the questions.

**Step 3**: Include a link to contents on your website that are related to the topic you are providing answers to within the comments.

Doing this helps you ride on the popularity and reputation of the forum. Search engines will be able to crawl your website, and your site's search engine reputation will also increase rapidly because it will be believed that your website contains useful content. Keep in mind that search engines treat each backlink as a vote so if you seem to be getting 'votes' from multiple sources within one forum or different forums, this will undoubtedly help.

3. **Social Bookmarking**: Social bookmarking also helps to improve your site's visibility to search engines. Social bookmarking is a web service that allows web users to save and share contents that they find interesting and useful on the web. It's almost like bookmarking a web page on your browser only that social bookmarking is done online and users can bookmark many pages. How to go about it:

**Step 1**: Search for popular social bookmarking websites. Some popular ones include StumbleUpon, Reddit, Delicious, and Digg. These are some of the best social bookmarking sites because they receive a lot of web traffic daily.

**Step 2**: Submit your web contents including blog posts and pages to each of the bookmarking sites frequently.

4. **Photo and Video sharing**: You must have seen one or two viral videos recently whether on social media or on the general web. Photo and video sharing is one of the effective ways to improve site SEO unlike in the past when it was only about articles. You can share images and photos related to your website content on photo sharing sites such as Photo Bucket, Flicker, and Picasa. When people see these photos which would include links to your site, they are able to share them, like them, and comment on them. Some people would even visit your site by following the links in the photo.

Just like photos, you can also share videos on sites like Vimeo and YouTube.

How to go about it:

**Step 1**: Create a business page for your website or your blog on YouTube, Vimeo etc.

**Step 2**: Convert some of your contents to videos. You can find freelancers online (Fiverr.com, Freelancer.com and Upwork.com are good examples) to do this for you easily.

**Step 3**: Write a description for the video, and make sure it includes links to your website.

**Step 4**: Continue to upload videos on video sharing websites.

You can get a lot of web traffic this way because Google search engines also includes videos in its results and many people prefer video contents to reading as videos tend to be more interesting to watch.

5. **Business Reviews**: If you are trying to promote your business website, business reviews can help to increase your visibility and ranking. You can ask bloggers or friends to write reviews about your business on business review sites like Stylefeeder, RateitAll, and Kaboodle.

These reviews should include links to your website so as to increase online reputation for your business.

6. **Social Shopping Networks:** If you're running an e-commerce website, you can increase visibility for your business by submitting your products to social shopping networks such as MSN Online Shopping, Yahoo Online Shopping, and Google Product Search.

This is a free advertising and link building strategy for e-commerce websites.

SEO with off-page strategy is incomplete SEO. As you continue to work hard to build the reputation of your business from within, you shouldn't neglect the outside world because doing so is leaving too much potential web traffic and search engine visibility on the table.

# I need your help...

We have come to the end of the book. Thank you for reading and congratulations for reading until the end.

Earlier, we mentioned that how fast or slow, how friendly your site is (to readers and search crawlers), your bounce rate, and other site factors such as social signals and mobile friendliness affect how well your page ranks on Google and other search engines.

Even if you do everything discussed here, if you fail to make your site search engine and user friendly, if you fail to improve your site speed, internal linking, and other factors such as mobile friendliness, you will be shooting yourself in the foot because even after creating a healthy keyword and backlink profile, your site will not rank first.

If you get right the things we have discussed in this book, I guarantee that your internet-marketing plan is going to take off faster than anything you know.

If you found the book valuable, can you recommend it to others? One way to do that is to post a review on Amazon.

I want to reach as many people as I can with this book, and more reviews will help me accomplish that!

If you have any questions or problems, please contact us: hello@freedomdestination.com.

Thank you and good luck!

# Preview Of 'Online Business from Scratch'

## Step 1: Why do you want to build an online business and why do people fail to build one successfully?

First, let me ask you a question. What does your dream life look like? Imagine that you're totally free. You don't have a 9-5 job, you don't have a boss. You can live wherever you want. You can do whatever you want. Imagine that. What would you do? You're able to travel the world, or you can spend all your time with your family. What is the most important thing to you? Please don't just read these questions, answer them too. Why do I ask these silly questions? Because building an online business requires hard work. So you need a 'why'. You need something that can motivate you when you have failures or just simply have a hard time. So first you need to know why you want to build an online business, what is your goal with it? It can be anything that can motivate you.

But why an online business? Today's world is all about technology and the internet. In fact, building an online business is easier, cheaper, and more profitable than building an offline business. You don't have to rent an office and pay a lot of money for offline advertising. You can start your own business with very little cost. However, you'll be able to make much more money than in an offline business in a much shorter period of time.

Last but not least, an online business can create a passive income so that you can live free. An online business can be automated. I think this is the most attractive reason. You might have to do some work with it, but you can work from wherever you want.

That's enough. I'm sure you already know what the advantages of building an online business are if you bought this book. So let's go over the next question, why do people fail to build a successful online business?

First, I want to clarify that failure isn't a bad thing. Failure is a natural thing and an opportunity to learn from your mistakes. Every successful person has failed and struggled at some point. Being successful is not easy. If it were easy, everybody would be successful. I know you saw so many ads about create millions without any work or any time. But that's not the reality. If you want to build something successful, you have to be patient. It isn't a fast process. Just think about a few successful people. They failed sometimes but they never gave up, that's why they achieved their goals. While some people give up when they encounter obstacles, the successful people stand up and learn from their mistakes.

Secondly, there's a lot of work to being successful. You have to put in the work. I don't care if you have a full-time job, I don't care if you have no time. Let's find a way to work as much on your online business as possible. If your goal is strong enough, I'm sure you can put in the work. You cannot be lazy.

My next advice is to have faith. You have to believe that you can do it. Read success stories. Find people who have already achieved what you want. If they can make it, you can make it too. It's not a scam, it works. If you have faith, you will take action and taking action is the key to building a successful online business.

Okay, so commit yourself and think long-term. You won't be successful and rich by tomorrow. However, if you start working on your business today, you will be thankful for it even a year later. I will show you the map, the strategies, but you must work hard and take action.

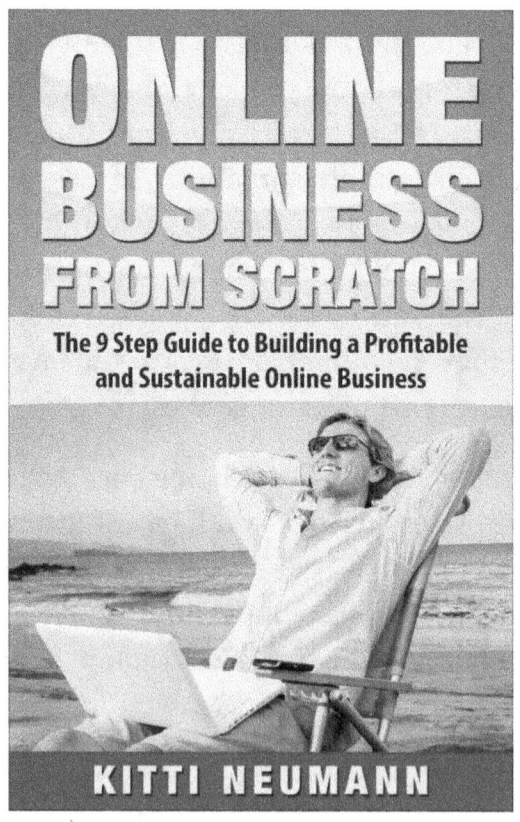

Check out the rest of Online Business from Scratch on Amazon or go to: http://amzn.to/2rH99A9

# Check Out My Other Books

Below you'll find some of my other popular books that are popular on Amazon and Kindle as well.

Alternatively, you can visit my author page on Amazon to see other work done by me.

**20 Easy And Fast Diet Tips For Losing Weight – An Easy-To-Follow Weight Loss Guide**

**Belly Diet: The Zero Belly Diet Step-By-Step Guide Which Will Help You To Lose Your Belly And Enjoy Your Flat Belly**

**Anti-Inflammatory Diet Guide – The Guide To Reduce Inflammation And Live A Healthy Life Without Pain**

**Dash Diet: Cookbook For Weight Loss With Action Plan And Easy Recipes**

**Clean Eating: Cookbook And Guide To Restore Your Body's Natural Balance And Eat Healthy**

**Negative Calorie Diet: Cookbook & Guide Which Help You To Burn Body Fat, Lose Weight And Live Healthy**

**Smart Fat: Cookbook With Fat Meals Which Help You To Lose Weight, Get Healthy And Improve Brain Function**

**Freedom: How To Make Money Online And Become Financially Free By Creating Passive Income**

**Negative Calorie Diet & Weight Loss Box Set**

**Leptin Resistance: Leptin Diet to Control Your Hormones, Get Permanent Weight Loss, Cure Obesity and Live Healthy**

**Online Business from Scratch: The 9 Step Guide to Building a Profitable and Sustainable Online Business**

**Freedom & Online Business from Scratch Box Set**

**Slow Cooker & Instant Pot Box Set**

**Negative Calorie Diet & Smart Fat Box Set**

**Negative Calorie Diet & Dash Diet Box Set**

**Negative Calorie Diet & Anti-Inflammatory Diet Guide Box Set**

**Negative Calorie Diet & Clean Eating Box Set**

**Instant Pot: Instant Pot Pressure Cooker Cookbook With Easy And Healthy Recipes**

**Slow Cooker: Cookbook with Slow Cooker Recipes**

**Psychology & Habits Of Highly Effective People Box Set**

**Psychology: How To Analyze People Using Human Psychological Techniques, Body Language Signals, Social Skills And Personality Types**

**Habits Of Highly Effective People: What Are The Habits Of Successful People?**

www.ingramcontent.com/pod-product-compliance
Lightning Source LLC
Chambersburg PA
CBHW071244220526
45468CB00002B/1000